Your Personal Motivation GPS

Portland, Oregon

Library of Congress Catalog Card Number: TXu002256912

ISBN: 978-0-9891727-4-5

Cover design by D Alexander Griffin

Manufactured in the United States of America

Ordering information:

Special discounts are available on quantity purchases. For details, visit:
afterball.net/books

Finding
Motivation?

Your M.A.P.S. To Motivation

By

D Alexander Griffin

To my boys, Diggy and Dash

CONTENTS

CONTENTS

Introduction

Have you been searching for the motivation to get started, or to keep going? It's a challenge I think we all have faced. Motivation comes in many ways, but the catalyst or spark that motivates you to act will be uniquely personal to you. What may motivate one person may make another person feel anxious or uninspired. Some people are motivated by a challenge with seemingly insurmountable odds, while others will be motivated to act is the "wins" are easy. Again, what gets you motivated to achieve a goal will be personal to you and only you.

Reading a few motivational words or phrases is sometimes all a person needs to be rejuvenated. Life's challenges can often leave one feeling as if there is no hope. Even if you have great intentions and a positive outlook on life, it's easy to feel that you've been "worked over."

Motivation comes in all shapes, sizes and experiences. What motivates you today, may not motivate you tomorrow. Or, during different times in your life, you may be motivated by different things. For example, people who choose to establish a career with a large and successful corporation may initially be motivated by the prospect of becoming wealthy. They dream of the accolades they will receive, the promotions, the corner office and so on. Then at some point along the way, as their career takes off, their motivations for working change. Now they may want a job that provided them with more time to spend with their families or more time to take vacations.

You may have heard the term "adrenaline junkie" – people who seek out intense, high-risk or thrilling activities that generate an adrenal rush. Feeling that boost of energy and heightened sense of awareness that comes when the hormone adrenaline is released into their blood is seemingly their sole motivation for doing anything. Then, something shifts for them. Their once insatiable need to find that next thrilling or risky adventure in order to feel alive eases a bit. They still want to feel alive and energized, but they start looking for a different or less risky path to get there.

The different ways you get to your motivation is liken to the different ways you might drive a car. You can drive in the fast lane or the slow lane. You can enjoy the scenery along the way or blow by it. There are rules you can observe, bend or break as you go. You can be on a long road trip or a short one. Or you can just stop at the light.

Your hands are on the steering wheel but your foot is on the pedal. That pedal is your motivation and it can take you anywhere you want to go.

About twenty years ago, a friend gave me a book entitled Acts of Faith – Daily Meditations For People Of Color, by Iyanla Vanzant. It was a turning point in my life. Acts of Faith had a powerful quote and saying for each day of the calendar year. The quotes were followed by a short story with real life scenarios, examples and life lessons. It seemed like each quote and story spoke directly to me and was exactly what I needed that day.

I had always thought I was a pretty positive person. But like many of us, I was often really hard on myself and I sometimes thought nothing was going quite right.

Well, I'm still reading this book and, even though I'm now familiar with the book's messages, whatever passage I read is still always appropriate for whatever I am experiencing in life.

Over the years, I've collected other motivational and self-help books so I would have them at my fingertips whenever I needed a "pick-me-up." I was so moved by a piece of advice I came across, that I continue to strive to follow it every day: "be the most positive person you know" by H. Jackson Brown Jr.

Now, I felt I had mastered the art of being positive until I met a person at one of my jobs; we'll call her Queen Positive, who seemed to me to be the most positive person on the planet. At that time, our sales team was male dominant and our accounts were as well. Queen P had an uphill battle with every conversation she would have with the accounts. She had to work twice as hard as everyone else to negotiate and get the same things done. I thought this was a tough profession for her to be in and wondered at the time why she chose it.

We worked together for about two years and often our sale team would go out for lunch together. Queen P seemed to be having fun all the time and everything that happened, to her was "the greatest experience!" Every meal was "the best ever" and, for that matter, every movie "deserved an Oscar."

At first, I was exasperated when I was around this person. I kept thinking, "she can't be real." Gradually, I realized that this person was the "real deal." I've heard that one way to maintain a positive outlook is to surround yourself with people who also have a positive outlook on life. I found myself drawn to her positive energy and wanted to be that positive beacon for everyone that I came in contact with. Surely, if she could have a positive outlook on everything, then I could too.

In this book, I will share with you motivational quotes and sayings that I have collected through reading, listening and seeking to follow a positive path. I hope this collection of motivational quotes shared by leaders, poets, writers and cultural and political icons will help you get through a tough day, make you smile, and maybe even change your outlook on life.

Your life's focus is always moving and what motivates you to take action will, too.

In this book I will outline a pathway, a global positioning system (GPS), so to speak, to help you find what will motivate you to make the most of your life. I call it M.A.P.S. You will decide where you want to go – how fast or slowly you move is up to you. My hope is to that you will be inspired and learn what it is that will keep you moving towards your goals.

I believe that a gift of something positive is a gift of power.

-- D. Alexander Griffin

THERE ARE SO MANY WAYS TO CHANGE THE DIRECTION YOU ARE GOING.

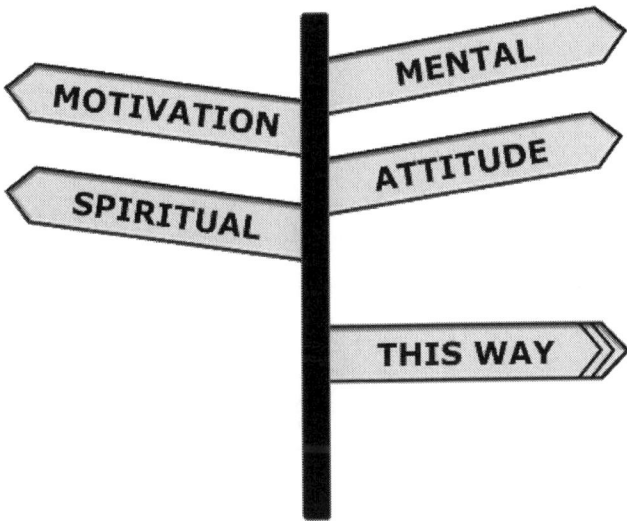

Definition of Motivation

HOW
  DOES
    THE
      WEBSTER
        DICTIONARY
        DEFINE
        THE
          WORD
            "MOTIVATION"?

Motivation (mo/te va/shen) 1. an act or instance of motivating. 2. the state of being motivated. 3. something that motivates; inducement; incentive.

What Is My Definition Of "MOTIVATION"?

Motivation is your **M.A.P.S.** to navigate towards a fulfilling life. Think for a minute what maps actually do for you. They help you find things you couldn't find yourself. They give you assurance about something you might already know. They get you out of jams that seem almost impossible to conquer. They give you the strength to start a quest and the confidence to finish it. They help you get where you need to be in life in a timely manner.

M = **Mental**

A = **Attitudinal**

P = **Physical**

S = **Spiritual**

Mental relates to the thoughts you hold in your mind. *Attitudinal* is the point of view or frame of make that you have. *Physical* relates to the actions you take. *Spiritual* relates to what moves you from a deep and perhaps unseen place.

You may think *mental* motivation and *attitudinal* motivation are fairly similar. Or that *physical* motivation and *spiritual* motivation are one and the same. In fact, these concepts do have similarities, but take on their own identities when you dig deeper.

For instance, the differences between mental and attitude is quite simple. Your *mental* motivation is what inspires you to get through the day-to-day life experiences. In contrast, your *attitudinal* motivation is your quick fix, or your immediate personal adjustment. *Mental* motivation is like eating protein with *attitudinal* motivation being a double shot of espresso in your soy caramel mocha, no whip.

Although there are similarities between *physical* motivation and *spiritual* motivation, they also have their differences. You have to feed your physical health as well as your spiritual health. Your *physical* motivation is your outside looking inward whereas your *spiritual* motivation is your inside looking out. Your *physical* motivation is 1 hour of running or circuit training with your *spiritual* motivation being one hour of prayer or meditation.

These different classifications of motivation are broken down further later in the book.

Mental Is Your
Motivational **Thoughts**.

Attitude Is Your
Motivational **Actions**.

Physical Is Your **Body**
Motivation.

Spiritual Is Your **Soul**
Motivation.

The Fear of Success

I heard people say that what motivates them is the fear of failure. Some individuals may think that if they fail at a task or if they are not able to achieve their goals, then there must be something wrong with them or that others will see them as being inadequate or just not good enough to find success in their lives. I'm not here to tell you that one motivational pathway is better or worse than another. I just want to encourage you to dig deeper into why certain things motivate you to take action and grow towards your dreams and other things may not.

Ask yourself whether your decision to try something new depends on your belief that you will succeed or fail? Do you dread failing so much that you will do anything not to fail? Are you so worried about what other people think that inaction feels better than taking an action where the outcome or your success is an unknown? Do you feel as if you would be letting, not only yourself, but everyone around you down if you were to fail at the task?

Motivation disguises itself in many ways. How you draw upon it is unique to every individual. What motivates one person may drive another person toward feelings of depression.

Holding on to something negative to motivate you could cause adverse effect in the long term. Let's look at revenge. Something physically or mentally traumatic may have happened to you or someone may have done something to you that you believe is so egregious, that it consumes your every thought.

Maybe you're a member of a soccer team and you believe your team lost a game and it was your fault. And on top of that, the opposing team made sure they rubbed it in as much as they could. Maybe you were bullied in your youth and you were never able to even the score. Or you were passed over for a job promotion that you knew you were qualified for. Or someone physically hurt you or someone in your family.

Holding on to negative thoughts can be agonizing and debilitating. These thoughts may keep you up at night. You may not be able to go about your everyday activities because you just can't get these thoughts out of your mind. You may even think getting revenge is the only way to get back to your normal self. But I would suggest that you ask yourself, "do I want to hold on to this kind of energy? Do you want a negative experience to be the fuel that moves me to act?" It's a question you have to look inside yourself to answer.

I believe revenge is only a temporary and hollow motivation. And let's say you work tirelessly for years to get yourself in position to take your revenge on a person or an entity that you believe has wronged you. What happens when you get to the end of this journey? Most of the time you will be left feeling empty. Why? Because the started the journey for the wrong reasons. You may even lose sight of the enriching and positive things you've accomplished during the journey because your ultimate goal was not for the betterment of yourself, your family or humanity.

It was just to cover up the hurt you have been feeling. Moreover, the person or persons whom you believe committed the wrong against you may not have spent a minute thinking about what has been hurting you for so long. For sure, the words or actions that triggered this hurt has long since passed into the wind. You are the only one still carrying this baggage from the past. So, you have to ask yourself, will taking revenge really be worth it? There is a chance the answer is "yes," but in most cases it's likely a resounding no.

What motivates you to act can be a tricky ally. If what motivates you is only fear of failing or not responding to an adverse situation, then you will never have the success that you so deeply want. Your motivations can be your most powerful allies. And with that power comes the responsibility to use it wisely.

Let's look at motivation from another angle. Some people, unknowingly have a fear of success. Take a minute to let that sink in. Deep down we know we can accomplish great things, but something is holding us back. And then procrastination sets in. We tell ourselves, "I know I can do it, so I'll just start tomorrow or next week." Or, "I could start now, but I don't have the time." Or, "I'm not ready to commit myself fully to my goal, but once I do, I know I'll accomplish it." These are common things we tell ourselves. We think there is always tomorrow or there will be a perfect time to get started.

The truth is, if we are waiting for that perfect time it will never come. Sometimes we complete the preliminary work that's necessary to achieve our goals and we will feel good about starting, but we never get to the finish line. We may even dream about what success will feel like and we'll find comfort in knowing that we've done some work and we can finish it at any time. Maybe the feeling of future success is enough to keep us committed to our goal.

This is more common than not. How many people you know that have a script that is sitting on their desk that no one else has seen? Or a book that they have started or even completed that they have not sent to a publisher. How many people have trained to run a marathon, but have never signed up for the race? You've heard people talk about their million-dollar idea, but few have pursued it. It's not because they don't want a million dollars. Instead, it could be that they fear of success.

I went to college on a track and field scholarship. Track and field wasn't my first favorite sport but over time, it became the sport I loved. I dreamed about winning the big race. I trained for years to prepare myself to compete at the highest level. I was in the weight room constantly. I never missed a practice. I even learned to meditate to so I could be become stronger mentally and begin envisioning what it would feel like to cross the finish line as a winner. But the opportunities I had to achieve my goals would come swiftly and go away even more swiftly.

There was always some reason I could not perform as well as I would have liked when it mattered most. When the stakes weren't as high, I would run personal bests. I would place first in the smaller races, but when the big races came, I could never run as fast as I knew I could. I would tell myself, if I had just run close to my best times, I would have won. I didn't think I was "choking" But my performances told me something else. I was never afraid of my competition, and I would run brilliantly for 3 quarters of my races. Then something would happen. I would think about how tiered I was, my form would break and it felt like I was running in quicksand or even backward. I was afraid of success.

This realization changed my life and the trajectory of my athletic accomplishments. I started to believe I deserved to have success. I started to believe that success was a result of the hard work I put in. I thought if I am working this hard, I deserve to reap the benefits. I wasn't afraid to do everything I could to train so why shouldn't I do everything I could to win. Experts say to find that one thing that motivates you and hold on to it with everything you've got.

Being afraid of success is like having an invisible crutch. It's like having a built-in excuse. I thought if I just ran harder, I would have won. If I was feeling 100%, I would have been able to push myself further and that would have catapulted me to the finish line. I was afraid of giving everything I had and not knowing what would happen.

When I was able to overcome the fear of not knowing what would happen if I gave it my all, the crutch fell off. The excuses started to disappear. And the success I dreamed about started to come to fruition.

There are no secrets to success. It is the result of preparation, hard work and learning from failure.

-- Colin Powell

M = MENTAL

Mental (men/tl) *(Merriam-Webster)*

1. Of or pertaining to the mind.

2. Of, pertaining to, or affected by a disorder of the mind: a mental patient.

3. For persons with a psychiatric disorder: a mental hospital.

4. Performed by or existing in the mind: mental arithmetic.

5. Pertaining to intellectuals or intellectual activity.

6. Informal. Insane; crazy.

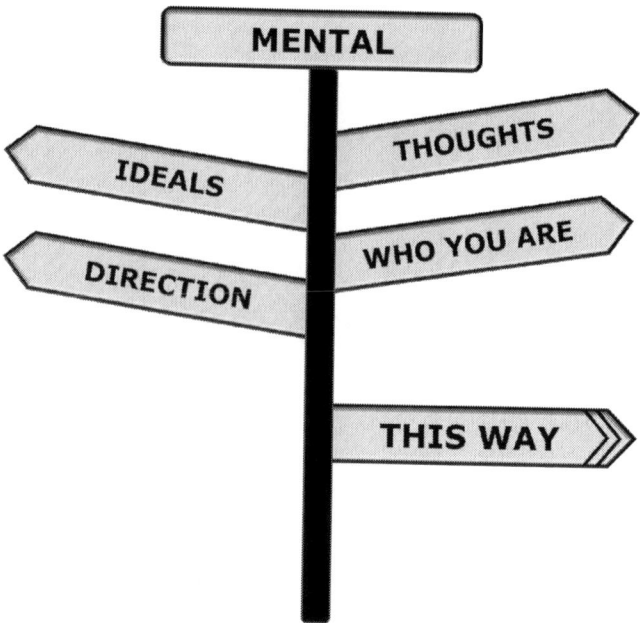

Mental is a culmination of your thoughts. When people ask questions about your mental wellbeing, what they are really asking is, are your inner thoughts uplifting or destructive.

"There is never a point in time when there is nothing on your mind." This is a statement that I believe in 100 percent. So, if this is the case, we are always engaged in supporting or undermining our mental wellbeing. Take for instance the old saying "never say I can't only I can." Or, "You can talk yourself in or out of anything." Positive thoughts repeated over and over in your mind will often create a positive feeling or outcome. Similarly, negative thoughts repeated over and over will create negative feelings or outcomes as well.

Saying someone is mental could be the best comment you could ever make about him or her.

How to get motivated:

Different people I encounter often come to me and ask; how do you get yourself motivated? They are looking for a few words that will change their world. Everyone is motivated by different things. So, I usually start the conversation with questions that help them reflect on themselves first. Only you know what motivates you. And, that thing could change depending on your mood, circumstances, goals and your history.

Finding your motivation doesn't always get you going, sometimes you have to get going to find your motivation.

There is a saying that you just need to get started and let the motivation catch up with you.

Here are 10 things (plus 1) you should think about in your journey towards motivation:

1. Remind yourself of why your goals are important to you.
2. Start with small ideas and let them grow into something big
3. Block out the daily distractions to better focus on your goals.
4. Find trusted people in your life to hold you accountable.
5. Get motivation from people who have already achieved a similar goal.
6. If you are looking for a quick boost, use music to give you energy.
7. Find the bright points in your failures
8. Keep a log and compare yourself with yourself to see how far you've come
9. Be grateful for where you are.
10. Remember your goals are not set in stone but are forever changing, adjust your goals accordingly.
11. And always, make sure you celebrate your successes.

Mental Quotes

Mental quotes stimulate the mind and gets your thinking in the right place

Motivation

People often say that motivation doesn't last. Well, neither does bathing – that's why we recommend it daily.

-- Zig Ziglar

Identification with an organization or a cause is no substitute for self-realization.

-- Swami Rudrananda

It takes a deep commitment to change and an even deeper commitment to grow.

-- Ralph Ellison

People often say that motivation doesn't last. Well, neither does bathing; that's why we recommend it daily.

-- Anonymous

What is now proved was once only imagined.

-- William Blake

The ablest man I ever met is the man you think you are.

-- Franklin D. Roosevelt

Practice hope. As hopefulness becomes a habit, you can achieve a permanently happy spirit.

-- Norman Vincent Peale

When you do nothing, you feel overwhelmed and powerless. But when you get involved, you feel the sense of hope and accomplishment that comes from knowing you are working to make things better.

-- Pauline R. Kezer

The greatest regrets in our lives are the risks we did not take. If you think something will make you happy, go for it. Remember that you pass this way only once!

-- Unknown

Have the courage to say no. Have the courage to face the truth. Do the right thing because it is right. These are the magic keys to living your life with integrity.

-- W. Clement Stone

All of life is an experiment. The more experiments you make, the better.

-- Ralph Waldo Emerson

The important thing is this: to be able at any moment to sacrifice what we are for what we could become.

-- Charles du Bois

If you always do what you always did, you will always get what you always got.

-- Jackie "Moms" Mabley

Dream as if you'll live forever. Live as if you'll die today.

-- James Dean

Dreams can often become challenging, but challenges are what we live for.

-- Travis White

To dream anything that you want to dream, that is the beauty of the human mind. To do anything that you want to do, that is the strength of the human will. To trust yourself, to test your limits, that is the courage to succeed.

-- Bernard Edmonds

Whatever you can do, or dream you can, begin it. Boldness has genius, power, and magic in it.

-- Johann Wolfgang von Goethe

The tragedy of life is not that it ends so soon, but that we wait so long to begin it.

-- Anonymous

It is one of the most beautiful compensations of life that no man can sincerely try to help another without helping himself.

-- Ralph Waldo Emerson

Today, I will be too calm for worry, too noble for anger and too strong for defeat. Today, I will believe anything is possible...

-- Christian D. Larson

The most important thing about motivation is goal setting. You should always have a goal. [???]

-- Francie Larrieu Smith

Every day brings 86,400 seconds. Whatever isn't used is lost forever.

-- Unknown

We tend to forget that happiness doesn't come as a result of getting something we don't have, but rather of recognizing and appreciating what we do have.

-- Fredrick Koeing

The very least you can do in your life is to figure out what you hope for. And the most you can do is live inside that hope. Not admire it from a distance but live right in it, under its roof.

-- Barbara Kingsolver

"I was thinking one day and I realized that if I just had somebody behind me all the way to motivate me, I could make a big difference. Nobody came along like that so I just became that person for myself."
--Unknown

A journey of a thousand miles begins with a single step.

-- Chinese Proverb

Concern should drive us into action and not into depression.

-- Karen Horney

He who waits to do a great deal of good at once, will never do anything.

-- Samuel Johnson

Happiness...it lies in the joy of achievement, in the thrill of creative effort.

--Franklin D. Roosevelt

Cherish your yesterdays, dream your tomorrows, but live your todays.

-- Unknow

Let the beauty we love be what we do.

-- Rumi

Happiness lies not in the mere possession of money; it lies in the joy of achievement, in the thrill of creative effort.

--Franklin D. Roosevelt

If you have built castles in the air, your work need not be lost. That is where they should be. Now put the foundation under them.

-- Henry David Thoreau

History has demonstrated that the most notable winners usually encountered heartbreaking obstacles before they triumphed. They won because they refused to become discouraged by their defeats.

-- Bertie C. Forbes

Mind

You have powers you never dreamed of. You can do things you never thought you could do. There are no limitations in what you can do except the limitations of your own mind.

-- Darwin P. Kingsley

Only those who risk going too far can possibly find out how far one can go.

-- T.S. Eliot

Success is to laugh often and much, to win the respect of intelligent people and the affection of children; to earn the appreciation of honest critics and endure the betrayal of false friends; to appreciate beauty; to find the best in others; to leave the world a bit better; to know even one life has breathed easier because you have lived. This is to have succeeded.

-- Ralph Waldo Emerson

Man cannot discover new oceans unless he has the courage to lose sight of the shore.

-- Andre Gide

If you chase two rabbits, both will escape.

-- Prover

We have to move beyond the mind-set of power-lessness.

-- Audrey Edwards

Happiness is not something you postpone for the future; it is something you design for the present.

-- Jim Rohn

Hold yourself responsible to a higher standard than anyone else expects of you. Never excuse yourself.

-- Henry Ward Beecher

Don't let yesterday use up too much of today. The best way to pay for a lovely moment is to enjoy it.

-- Richard Bach

"Make sure your worst enemy doesn't live between your own two ears."

-- Laird Hamilton

An education isn't how much you have committed to memory, or even how much you know. It's being able to differentiate between what you know and what you don't.

-- Anatole France

Impossibilities are merely things which we have not yet learned.

-- Charles W. Chesnutt

Most people are about as happy as they make up their minds to be.

-- Anonymous

It is what we think we know already that often prevents us from learning.

-- Claude Bernard

Perseverance is a great element of success. If you only knock long enough and loud enough at the gate, you are sure to wake up somebody.

-- Henry Wadsworth Longfellow

Give help rather than advice.

-- Luc de Vauvenargues

The optimist proclaims that we live in the best of all possible worlds; and the pessimist fears this to be true.

-- James Branch Cabell

Imagination is more important than knowledge.

-- Albert Einstein

All the powers in the universe are already ours. It is we who have put our hands before our eyes and cry that it is dark.

-- Swami Vivekananda

We probably wouldn't worry about what people think of us if we could know how seldom they do.

-- Olin Miller

The quality, not the longevity, of one's life is what is important.

-- Dr. Martin Luther King, Jr.

When one door closes another door opens; but we so often look so long and so regretfully upon the closed door, that we do not see the ones which open for us.

-- Alexander Graham Bell

You must begin wherever you are.

-- Jack Boland

Being defeated is often a temporary condition. Giving up is what makes it permanent.

-- Marilyn vos Savant

If at first you don't succeed, you are running about average.

-- M.H. Alderson

You can accomplish by kindness what you cannot do by force.

-- Publilius Syrus (1st century BC)

The abundance you desire to experience must first be an experience in your mind. [Mental?]

-- Ernest Holmes

When self-respect takes its rightful place in the psyche, you will not allow yourself to be manipulated by anyone.

-- Indira Mahindra

Do not attempt to do a thing unless you are sure of yourself; but do not relinquish it simply because someone else is not sure of you.

-- Stewart E. White

We judge ourselves by what we feel capable of doing, while others judge us by what we have already done.

-- Longfellow

We must accept finite disappointment, but we must never lose infinite hope.

-- Dr. Martin Luther King, Jr.

In the province of the mind, what one believes to be true either is true or becomes true.

-- John Lilly

If you have no confidence in self, you are twice defeated in the race of life. With confidence, you have won even before you have started.

-- Marcus Garvey

Thought

Happiness is a conscious choice, not an automatic response.

-- Mildred Barthel

It is not easy to find happiness in ourselves, and it is not possible to find it elsewhere.

-- Agnes Repplier

To be who you are and become what you are capable of is the only goal worth living.

-- Alvin Ailey

You must realize what is actually going on before you can effectively deal with it.

-- Ralpha

Praise, like gold and diamonds, owes its values only to its scarcity.

-- Samuel Johnson

Imagination is the beginning of creation. You imagine what you desire; you will what you imagine and at last you create what you will.

-- George Bernard Shaw

If you have learned how to disagree without being disagreeable, then you have discovered the secret of getting along – whether it be business, family relations, or life itself.

-- Bernard Meltzer

Did you ever see an unhappy horse? Did you ever see a bird that had the blues? One reason why birds and horses are not unhappy is because they are not trying to impress other birds and horses.

-- Dale Carnegie

Always look at what you have left. Never look at what you have lost.

-- Robert H. Schuller

Common sense is the knack of seeing things as they are, and doing things as they ought to be done.

-- Harriet Beecher Stowe

The best way to have a good idea is to have lots of ideas.

-- Linus Pauling

Examine the labels you apply to yourself. Every label is a boundary or limit you will not let yourself cross.

-- Dwayne Dyer

Life doesn't have to be a strain or struggle.

-- Marion Anderson

In my life, I have found there are two things about which I should never worry. First, I shouldn't worry about the things I can't change. If I can't change them, worry is certainly most foolish and useless. Second, I shouldn't worry about the things I can change. If I can change them, then taking action will accomplish far more than wasting my energies in worry. Besides, it is my belief that, 9 times out of 10, worrying about something does more danger than the thing itself. Give worry its rightful place - out of your life.

-- Unknown

We have to learn to be our own best friends because we fall too easily into the trap of being our own worst enemies.

-- Roderick Thorpe

The art of living does not consist in preserving and clinging to a particular mood or happiness, but in allowing happiness to change its form without being disappointed by the change; for happiness, like a child, must be allowed to grow up.

-- Charles Langbridge Morgan

Some men see things as they are and ask why. Others dream things that never were and ask why not.

-- George Bernard Shaw

You can complain because roses have thorns, or you can rejoice because thorns have roses.

-- ZIGGY

Leadership is doing what is right when no one is watching.

-- George Van Valkenburg

Even though you may want to move forward in your life, you may have one foot on the brakes. In order to be free, we must learn how to let go. Re- lease the hurt. Release the fear. Refuse to entertain your old pain. The energy it takes to hang onto the past is holding you back from a new life. What is it you would let go of today?

-- Mary Manin Morrissey

LESSON OF THE DOG

If a dog were your teacher, you would learn things like:

- When loved ones come home, always run to greet them.

- Never pass up the opportunity to go for a joyride.

- Allow the experience of fresh air and the wind in your face to be pure ecstasy.

- When it's in your best interest, practice obedience.

- Let others know when they've invaded your territory.

- Take naps and stretch before rising.

- Run, romp, and play daily.

- Thrive on attention and let people touch you.

- Avoid biting when a simple growl will do.

- On warm days, stop to lie on your back on the grass.

- On hot days, drink lots of water and lie down under a shady tree.

- When you're happy, dance around and wag your entire body.

- No matter how often you're scolded, don't buy into the guilt thing and pout; run right back and make friends.

- Delight in the simple joy of a long walk.

- Eat with gusto and enthusiasm. Stop when you have had enough.

- Be loyal.

- Never pretend to be something you're not.

- And most of all... If what you want lies buried, dig until you find it.

-- Unknown

DOGS ON PREMISES

If man hasn't discovered something that he will die for, he isn't fit to live.

-- Dr. Martin Luther King, Jr.

Change starts when someone sees the next step.

-- William Drayton

Difficult times have helped me to understand better than before, how infinitely rich and beautiful life is in every way, and that so many things that one goes worrying about are of no importance whatsoever.

-- Isak Dinesen

The best years of your life are the ones in which you decide your problems are your own. You do not blame them on your mother, the ecology or the president. You realize that you control your own destiny.

-- Albert Ellis

You have no control over what the other guy does. You only have control over what you do.

-- A.J. Kitt

He that never changes his opinion, never corrects his mistakes, will never be wiser on the morrow than he is today.

-- Tyron Edwards

You don't own the future you don't own the past. Today is all you have.

-- Les Brown

If you want happiness for an hour – take a nap. If you want happiness for a day – go fishing. If you want happiness for a month – get married. If you want happiness for a year – inherit a fortune. If you want happiness for a lifetime – help someone else.

-- Chinese proverb

If you follow your bliss, you put yourself on a kind of track, which has been there all the while waiting for you, and the life that you ought to be living is the one you are living.

-- Joseph Campbell

When I examine myself and my methods of thought, I come close to the conclusion that the gift of fantasy has meant more to me than talent for absorbing positive knowledge.

-- Albert Einstein

When you take charge of your life, there is no longer a need to ask permission of other people or society at large. When you ask permission, you give someone veto power over your life.

-- Geoffrey F. Abert

Four things come not back – the spoken word, the sped arrow, the past life and the neglected opportunity.

-- Arabian Proverb

Failure "Not" Fear "Not"

Our deepest fear is not that we are in- adequate. Our deepest fear is that we are powerful beyond measure. It is our light, not our darkness, that most frightens us.

-- Nelson Mandela

No one ever won a chess game by betting on each move. Sometimes you have to move backward to get a step forward.

-- Amar Gopal Bose

Our doubts are traitors, and make us lose the good that we oft may win, by fearing to attempt.

-- William Shakespeare

It takes but one positive thought when given a chance to survive and thrive to overpower an entire army of negative thoughts.

-- Robert H. Schuller

Failure is only the opportunity to more intelligently begin again.

-- Henry Ford

What would you attempt to do if you knew you could not fail?

-- Anonymous

Courage is a special kind of knowledge: the knowledge of how to fear what ought to be feared & how not to fear what ought not to be feared.

-- David Ben-Gurion

It is hard to fail, but it is worse never to have tried to succeed. In this life we get nothing save by effort.

-- Theodore Roosevelt

Failure is only a temporary change in direction to set you straight for your next success.

-- Denis Waitley

He who fears something gives it power over him.

-- Moorish Proverb

The toughest thing about being a success is the you've got to keep on being a success.

-- Irving Berlin

The greatest mistake you can make is to be continually fearing you will make one.

-- Elbert Hubbard

Restlessness is discontent and discontent is the first necessity of progress. Show me a thoroughly satisfied man-and I will show you a failure.

-- Thomas Edison

Confidence comes not from always being right but from not fearing to be wrong.

-- Peter T. McIntyre

Even death is not to be feared by one who has lived wisely.

-- Siddhartha Gautama

Hatred is never anything but fear – if you feared no one, you would hate no one.

-- Hugh Downs

Failure is not the worst thing in the world. The very worst is not to try.

-- Anonymous

One of the reasons people stop learning is that they become less and less willing to risk failure.

-- John W. Gardner

Do not fear to step into the unknown for where there is risk, there is also reward.

-- Lori Hard

Pride attaches undue importance to the superiority of one's status in the eyes of others; and shame is fear of humiliation of one's inferior status in the estimation of others. When one sets his heart on being highly esteemed and achieves such rating, then he is automatically involved in fear of losing his status.

-- Lao-Tzu

If you fear making anyone mad, then you ultimately probe for the lowest common denominator of human achievement.

-- James Earl "Jimmy" Carter, Jr.

He who is not every day conquering some fear has not learned the secret of life.

-- Ralph Waldo Emerson

You can make more friends in two months by becoming interested in other people than you can in two years by trying to get other people interested in you.

-- Dale Carnegie

A person's true wealth is the good he or she does in the world.

-- Mohammed

Just Get Started

"Catching up with time!"

Do you ever feel like life is speeding by and you just can't catch up with it? That's a feeling we all may have had at different times in our lives. We think that if we could just slow time down a bit, we could get our feet under us and start working towards our goals.

One of my favorite quotes is "Start where you are. Use what you have. Do what you can." That quote is from Arthur Ash. He did amazing things on and off of the tennis court. Arthur graduated 1st in his class in high school. He is the only black male tennis player to win Wimbledon and the U.S. Open. Arthur was the first (and only) African-American to be ranked #1 in the world. He received honorary doctorates from numerous higher institutions during his lifetime from Dartmouth College, LeMoyne-Owen College, Princeton University, Saint John's University, Trinity University, Hartford College, and Virginia Union University. And he was inducted into the Tennis Hall of Fame in 1985. These are just a few of his accomplishments over his lifetime.

There may never be the best time to start a project, cultivate an idea, create a prototype or go after your dreams. Every day you wait for the best or the right time, the right time gets farther away. Thus, giving you the feeling that you can't catch up. This quote from Mr. Ash illustrates the mentality and attitude you need to take that first step. What happens when you take a step? Once you take that first step you build momentum to keep moving forward. You may fall flat on your face but movement in a positive direction will eventually get you where you want to go.

You know this deep down, but something keeps you from starting down a road to get where you want to go. That road seems long, curvy and full of obstacles. It's dark and scary. If you can't see the end it's hard to believe there is an end.

This perception impedes your natural instincts to get started, it inhibited our growth. It kept you in a place that is comfortable. You are not doing the things you were meant to do, the things you are capable of. It keeps you stuck in the slow lane wondering how fast or far you could really go. It's part of human nature to go and eventually go faster and faster.

We may understand that things around us are moving at the speed of light but we are stuck with a snail's shell on our back. Success is moving forward without the guarantee of where we are going. Now this may make you feel anxious. Not only because of the fear of the unknown but also the fear that others have found a way to hop on the train that you missed. So, you wait for the next train and the next. Thinking that the right one, going to the right place with be the next train you see. Some people wait at the station their who life, missing what could be around the mountain or even just around the corner. Thinking that even if they jumped on the next train, they would still so far behind that we can't catch up.

Life is about hopping on that train. Having the confidence in yourself that wherever it's going, you'll be ready for it. It's what you've longed for, what you crave. And the only thing you need to do is take the first step. I could say just take the step but I know it's not that easy. I could say don't worry about where you're going but I know that's not how we operate. The ability to believe in something that can't be seen, heard or touched is not a natural function in our lives.

Sometimes what's around the corner is not great, it could bring immense challenges that could lead to heartbreak or despair. The ability to bounce back from failures is something people are never 100% sure of. Bounce back from small things is at least digestible, but bouncing back from things that are major or unknown is sometimes overwhelming. This is what keeps people from achieving great things. The great things we dream about. The bottom line is, maybe we can't catch up with time. But that doesn't matter. As long as we make the first step, we'll get there in plenty of time.

A = ATTITUDINAL

Attitude (at/i tood) *(Merriam-Webster)*

1. Manner, disposition, feeling, position, etc., with regard to a person or thing; tendency or orientation, esp. of the mind: a cheerful attitude.

2. position or posture of the body appropriate to or expressive of an action, emotion, etc.: to assume a threatening attitude.

3. the inclination of the three principal axes of an aircraft relative to the wind, to the ground, etc.

4. Slang. A testy, uncooperative disposition.

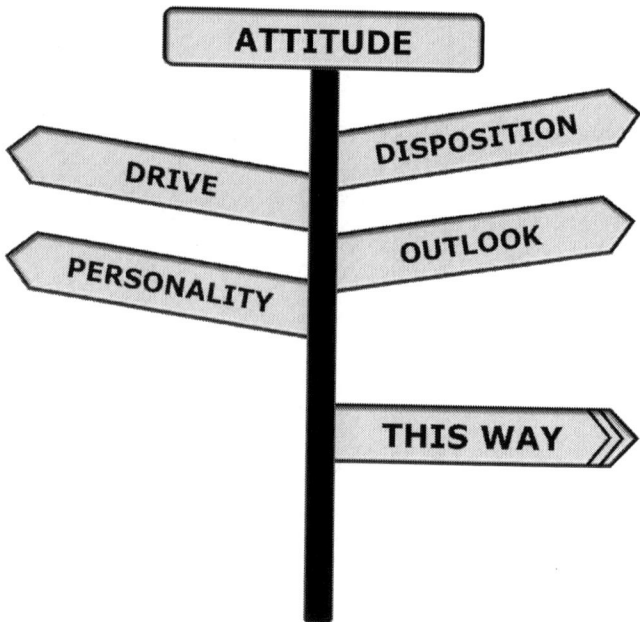

My definition of *attitudinal* motivation is basically *mental* motivation with crushed red peppers and habanera sauce. Your attitude is what drives you to do things. Your attitude is your ambition, desire and courage wrapped up in one big ball of fire. If Mental is your thoughts then Attitude is how you act them out.

Whether you have a positive attitude or a negative attitude, you better believe whichever one will probably map out the direction you going in. Attitudes, like any type of motivation can be controlled, directed and ultimately changed. Try thinking of something that puts a smile on your face. Within minutes you can't help but feel good about things.

Your attitude, not your aptitude, will determine your altitude.

-- Zig Ziglar

The Underdog

Why do we root for the underdog? There are many movies and documentaries that have the story of the underdog fighting through insurmountable odd to achieve their goals. Think about movies such as Rocky, Braveheart, The Karate Kid, Rudy, Remember the Titans, Miracle, Cool Runnings, 8 Mile, Million Dollar Baby, Slumdog Millionaire, Seabiscuit, Hoosiers, The Longest Yard, and so on.

These movies were successful in helping us identify with the characters. We learned about their lives, their challenges and were then able to see ourselves "in their shoes."

We identify with the characters in their quest to do big things when everyone around them doubted they could. The fact that the main characters in these movies didn't have the physical prowess of their competitors or the financial backing or even a level playing field on which to compete, yet they still persevered, gives us hope.

We might think, if they can do it, so can we. These examples of individuals overcoming the odds to achieve their goals are a form of validation. The motivation that drives us. It helps marginalizing our internal doubts that can keep us from taking that first step.

Sometimes it takes seeing someone else succeed when they are in a situation that is perceived to be worse than our own to motivate us to take action or change something in our lives.

When we hear stories of people that have overcome impossible odds it gives us the most important thing in the world.

It gives us hope...

This is why everyone loves an underdog story.

Attitude Quotes

Your attitude is the first line of defense ...and offense

Determination/Resilience

Deal with yourself as an individual worthy of respect and make everyone else deal with you the same way.

-- Nikki Giovanni

You may not know how to raise your self-esteem, but you definitely know how to stop lowering it.

-- Awo Osun Kunle

A man who stands for nothing will fall for anything.

-- El-Hajj Malik El Shabazz (Malcolm X)

The bumblebee's wings are so thin and its body is so big, it should not be able to fly. The only problem is, the bee doesn't know that.

-- David Lindsey

Instead of wallowing in my misery, I just made some changes.

-- Stephanie Mills

Ability is what you're capable of doing. Motivation determines what you do. Attitude determines how well you do it.

-- Lou Holtz

There are three kinds of people in the world: those who make things happen, those who watch things happen, those who wonder what happened.

-- Mary Kay Ash

The way to develop self-confidence is to do the thing you fear and get a record of successful experiences behind you. Destiny is not a matter of chance, it is a matter of choice; it is not a thing to be waited for, it is a thing to be achieved.

-- William Jennings Bryan

Be the change you want to see in the world.

-- Mohandas Gandhi

There are some people who live in a dream world, and there are some who face reality; and then there are those who turn one into the other.

-- Douglas Everett

Confidence is not trying the knob after you've locked the door.

-- William McFee

It's better to keep one's mouth shut and be thought a fool than to open it and resolve all doubt.

-- Abraham Lincoln

You must learn how to make it on the broken pieces.

-- Rev. Louise Williams-Bishop

"Be miserable. Or motivate yourself. Whatever has to be done, it's always your choice."
-- Wayne Dyer

Every man has three characters – that which he exhibits, that which he has, and that which he thinks he has.

-- Alphonse Karr

Live as if everything you do will eventually be known.

-- Hugh Prather

The day you take complete responsibility for yourself, the day you stop making any excuses, that's the day you start to the top.

-- O.J. Simpson

To dare is to lose one's footing momentarily. To not dare is to lose oneself.

-- Soren Kierkegaard

Don't give up what you want most

for what you want at the moment.

There are no shortcuts to any place worth going.

-- Beverly Sills

Fall seven times, stand up eight.

-- Japanese proverb

Even if you are on the right track, you'll get run over if you just sit there.

-- Will Rogers

You get what you expect.

-- Alvin Ailey

Act the way you want to be and soon you will be the way you act.

-- Dr. Johnnie Coleman

Life is like riding a bicycle. You don't fall off unless you plan to stop peddling.

-- Claude Pepper

Your world is as big as you make it.

-- Georgia Douglas Johnson

Attack life, it's going to kill you anyway.

-- Steven Coallier

You gain strength, courage and confidence by every experience in which you really stop to look fear in the face. You must do the thing which you think you cannot do.

-- Anna Eleanor Roosevelt

Opportunities are usually disguised as hard work, so most people don't recognize them.

-- Unknown

As long as you can find someone else to blame for anything you are doing you cannot be held accountable or responsible for your growth or lack of it.

-- Sun Bear

Courage is doing what you're afraid to do. There can be no courage unless you're scared.

-- Eddie Rickenbacker

Education is your passport to the future, for tomorrow belongs to the people who prepare for it to- day.

-- El-Hajj Malik El Shabazz (Malcolm X)

To be prepared is half the victory.

-- Miguel Cervantes

If you can't make a mistake, you can't make anything.

-- Marva Collins

He who does not hope to win has already lost.

-- Jose Joaquin Olmedo

What really matters is what you do with what you have.

-- Shirley Lord

If you have a great ambition, take as big a step as possible in the direction of fulfilling it. The step may only be a tiny one, but trust that it may be the largest one possible for now.

-- Mildred McAfee

If there is any kindness I can show, or any good thing I can do to any fellow being, let me do it now, and not deter or neglect it, as I shall not pass this way again.

-- William Penn

Whenever you are to do a thing, though it can never be known but to yourself, ask yourself how you would act were all the world looking at you and act accordingly.

-- Thomas Jefferson

The winners in life think constantly in terms of I can, I will, and I am. Losers, on the other hand, concentrate their waking thoughts on what they should have or would have done, or what they can't do.

-- Dennis Waitley

The smart ones ask when they don't know. And, sometimes when they do.

-- Malcolm Forbes

Make the most of yourself, for that is all there is of you.

-- Ralph Waldo Emerson

We all have ability. The difference is how we use it.

-- Stevie Wonder

Life has two rules: number 1, Never quit! number 2, always remember number 1.

-- Duke Ellington

If you're not living on the edge, you're taking up too much space.

-- Jim Whittaker

The best preparation for tomorrow is doing your best today.

-- Henry Jackson Brown

Those with a high level of confidence may have as many or more weaknesses than those with lower self-esteem. The difference is this; instead of dwelling on their handicaps, they compensate for them by dwelling on their strengths.

-- Alan Loy McGinnis

Be a first-rate version of yourself, not a second-rate version of someone else.

-- Judy Garland

We will either find a way or make one.

-- Hannibal

The only person who can stop me is me—and I can take her!

-- Anonymous

The future belongs to those who see possibilities before they become obvious.

-- John Sculley

You are what you think. You are what you go for. You are what you do!

-- Bob Richards

Life isn't worth living unless you're willing to take some big chances and go for broke.

-- Eliot Wiggington

Enthusiasm finds the opportunities, and energy makes the most of them.

-- Henry Hoskins

I don't possess a lot of self-confidence. I'm an actor so I simply act confident every time I hit the stage. I am consumed with the fear of failing.

Reaching deep down & finding confidence has made all my dreams come true.

-- Arsenio Hall

Example is not the main thing in influencing others; it is the only thing.

-- Bo Short

I've always felt it was not up to anyone else to make me give my best.

-- Akeem Olajuwon

Nothing in the world can take the place of persistence. Talent will not; nothing is more common than unsuccessful men with talent. Genius will not; un-rewarded genius is almost a proverb. Education will not; the world is full of educated derelicts. Persistence and determination alone are omnipotent. The slogan, "Press on," has solved and al- ways will solve the problems of the human race

-- Calvin Coolidge

People prefer to follow those who help them, not those who intimidate them.

-- C. Gene Wilkes

You cannot raise a man up by calling him down.

-- William Boetcker

This time like all times is a very good one if we but know what to do with it.

-- Ralph Waldo Emerson

Courage is your willingness to take action with no guarantee of results.

-- Brian Tracy

Look at a day when you are supremely satisfied at the end. It's not a day when you lounge around doing nothing; it's when you've had everything to do and you've done it.

-- Margaret Thatcher

Watch your thoughts;
they become words.
Watch your words;
they become actions.
Watch your actions;
they become habits.

Watch your habits;
they become character.
Watch your character;
it becomes your destiny.

-- Frank Outlaw

Encouragement/Inspiration

You cannot fix what you will not face.

-- James Baldwin

If you are on the road to nowhere, find another road.

-- Ashanti proverb

If you can believe it, the mind can achieve it.

-- Ronnie Lott

Do not wish to be anything but what you are, and to be that perfectly.

-- St. Francis De Sales

It is never too late to be what we might have been.

-- George Eliot

Whatever you want to do, do it now. There are only so many tomorrows.

-- Unknown

If we all did the things we are capable of; we would astound ourselves.

-- Thomas Edison

On life's journey faith is nourishment, virtuous deeds are a shelter, wisdom is the light by day and right mindfulness is the protection by night. If a man lives a pure life, nothing can destroy him.

-- Buddha

Youth is not a time of life, it is a state of mind. You are as old as your doubt, your fear, your despair. The way to keep young is to keep your faith young. Keep your self-confidence young. Keep your hope young.

-- Luella F. Phean

If you are feeling good about you, what you're wearing outside doesn't mean a thing.

--Leontyne Price

When I hear somebody sigh, "Life is hard," I am always tempted to ask, "Compared to what?"

--Sydney J. Harris

The ablest man I ever met is the man you think you are.

--Franklin D. Roosevelt

Everything you want is out there waiting for you to ask. Everything you want also wants you. But you have to take action to get it.

-- Jack Canfield

Do every act of your life as if it were your last.

-- Marcus Aurelius

The purpose of life, after all, is to live it, to taste experience to the utmost, to reach out eagerly and without fear for newer and richer experiences.

-- Anna Eleanor Roosevelt

With every wish that you make comes the power to make it come true. But it is up to you to provide the work that will make it a reality. Are you using your power to make your wishes come true today?

-- Libby Rosenauer

I am only one; but still I am one. I cannot do everything, but still I can do something. I will not refuse to do the something I can do.

-- Helen Keller

We make a living by what we get, but we make a life by what we give.

-- Norman MacEswan

What today will be like is up to me. I get to choose what kind of day I will have! Have a great day...unless you have other plans.

-- Ernest Murray

Go out and make people feel good for no good reason.

-- Richard Bandler

The best way to change your belief system is to change the truth about you. What you actually do is more important than what you say you'll do.

-- Steve Chandler

You have to have confidence in your ability, and then be tough enough to follow through.

-- Rosalynn Smith Carter

The greater part of our happiness or misery depends on our disposition and not our circumstances.

-- Anonymous

Don't dwell on reality; it will only keep you from greatness.

-- Rev. Randall R. McBride, Jr.

The best way to predict the future is to create it.

-- Unknown

No one can make you feel inferior without your consent.

-- Anna Eleanor Roosevelt

Striving for excellence motivates you; striving for perfection is demoralizing.

-- Harriet Braiker

The greater part of our happiness or misery depends on our disposition and not our circumstances.

-- Anonymous

Don't dwell on reality; it will only keep you from greatness.

-- Rev. Randall R. McBride, Jr.

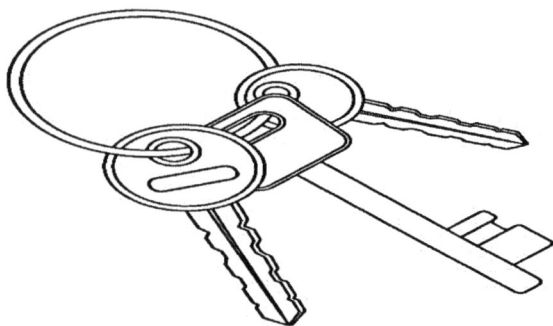

Keys to Success

Recipe for success: Study while others are sleeping; work while others are loafing; prepare while others are playing; and dream while others are wishing.

-- William A. Ward

Eighty percent of success is showing up.

--Woody Allen

People of mediocre ability sometimes achieve outstanding success because they don't know when to quit. Most men succeed because they are determined to.

-- George E. Allen

Keep in mind that neither success nor failure is ever final.

-- Roger W Babson

Your failures in life come from not realizing your nearness to success when you give up.

-- Yoruba proverb

Put your heart, mind, intellect and soul even to your smallest acts. This is the secret of success.

-- Swami Sivananda

Men succeed when they realize that their failures are the preparation for their victories.

-- Ralph Waldo Emerson

Be of good cheer. Do not think of today's failures, but of the success that may come tomorrow. You have set yourself a difficult task, but you will succeed if you persevere; and you will find a joy in overcoming obstacles.

-- Helen Keller

Success is not a destination that you ever reach. Success is the quality of your journey.

-- Jennifer James

People with goals succeed, because they know where they're going.

-- Earl Nightingate

Success is getting and achieving what you want. Happiness is wanting and being content with what you get.

-- Bernard Meltzer

A person's probability of success is directly proportional to the belief and execution of their abilities.

-- Kent Calhoun

Success is the sum of small efforts, repeated day in and day out.

-- Robert Collier

If you envy successful people, you create a negative force field of attraction that repels you from ever doing the things that you need to do to be successful. If you admire successful people, you create a positive force field of attraction that draws you toward becoming more and more like the kinds of people that you want to be like.

-- Brian Tracy

Success is to be measured not so much by the position that one has reached in life as by the obstacles which he has overcome while trying to succeed.

-- Booker T. Washington

There are no secrets to success. It is the result of preparation, hard work and learning from failure.

-- Colin Powell

Aim for success, not perfection. Never give up your right to be wrong, because then you will lose the ability to learn new things and move forward with your life. Remember that fear always lurks behind perfectionism. Confronting your fears and allowing yourself the right to be human can, paradoxically, make yourself a happier and more productive person.

-- Dr. David M. Burns

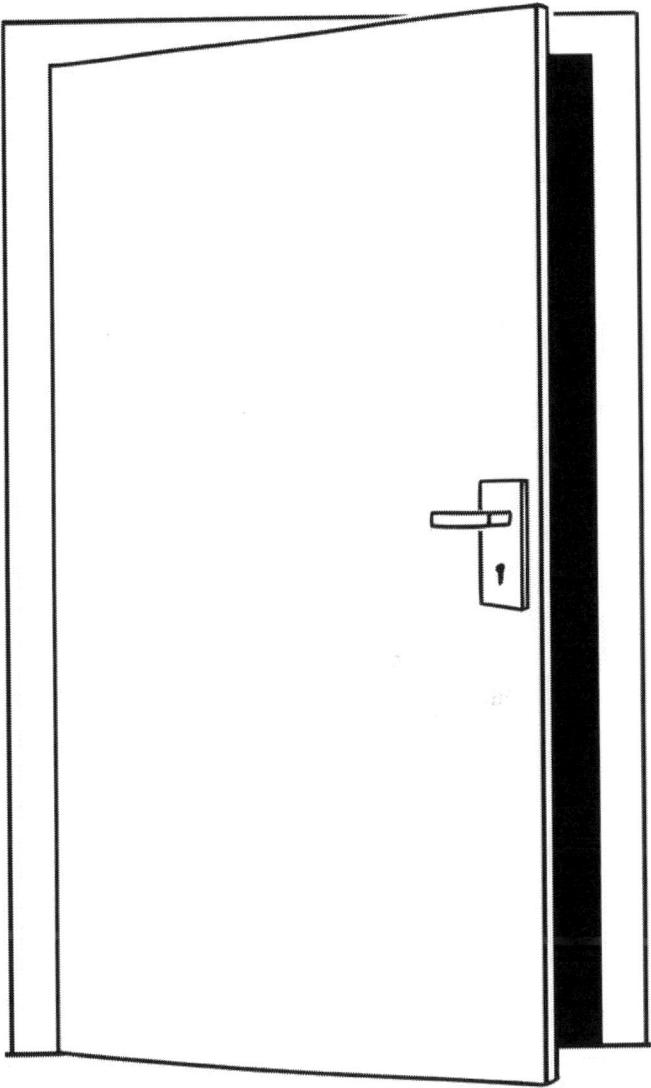

Success and failure

There is not much difference in people that succeed and people that fail. Some people are des- tined to succeed because they never think they could actually fail.

Another situation that haunts the best of us is, we are actually afraid to succeed. It stems from not believing we deserve success or not really knowing what to do once we get that success. It's far easier to live in the place we are than to shake it up and venture into something foreign to us.

Take for instance hitting the jackpot or winning the lottery, everyone wants to win the lottery. But if you really contemplate the reality of winning, it may not be as great as it looks.

For instance, take this scenario:

You hear stories of people that won the lottery and three years later they are back to where they started from and you wonder what were they thinking. You say if I had won, I could never blow 12 million dollars. But the fact of the matter is, are you really mentally ready to change your life completely.

Let's say you win the lottery. The first thing every-one says is that they will quit their job. It sounds great, but from the beginning you are changing the most comfortable routine you have. Whether you believe it or not, getting up in the morning and going to work or school still provides a feeling of comfort, even though you may feel like you hate it.

Bottom line is you might have to quit your job anyway because when your co-workers find out you hit the big one, they will have their hands out.

Next you will probably have to move to another neighborhood or another town because when your friends that live on the block find out, they will have their hands out.

Now that your home life has changed drastically, let's talk about when the relatives find out. You will have relatives that come out of the wood- works. You'll wind up feeling obligated to spend and share the wealth with your immediate and ex- tended family.

So, there you have it. Three years later you are back where you started from. This is not only be- cause of lack of vision but a subliminal desire to get back to the familiarity of the life you once had.

Don't get me wrong; I would love to win the lottery, but I just wanted to give you a little food for thought.

Goals

5 key steps to take to achieve your goals:

1. Focus on one goal at a time. If you are like me, you probably want to achieve all of you goals at once. I've found that this spreads you way too thin. While multitasking seems like you are getting more done, it can be counterproductive. The best way to complete a task is by taking time to focus your thoughts and energy on the task at hand until it is completed. Then you can move on to the next one.

2. Search for your motivation. Whether it's the feeling of accomplishment, success, monetary stability or fame. Whatever it is that motivates you, visualize it, seek it out and embrace it to the fullest. Remember motivation comes in many different ways and it's something that you need to continue to incorporate in your journey towards your goals.

3. Post your goals in as many places you can. You need to see your goals all of the time to continue to focus on them. Strategically place reminders in all aspects of your daily routine of your goals in plain sight. This will consciously and subconsciously ingrain them in your mindset. It will also build anticipation of you completing your goals and the spoils that go with them.

4. Socialize your goals. That's right tell your family, friends and anyone that will listen what your goals are. You may find the people you

communicate your goals to may have some knowledge, tips or connections that could help or support you in your journey. Never be afraid to solicit help. It's hard to accomplish something alone.

5. Never give up. There will always be ebbs and flows and they say when one door closes another one opens. Keep an open mind and stay resilient. There will always be negative thoughts that creep in your mind. Replace those thoughts with positive ones. Build on and cherish the small advancements or successes. Know that any goal, at any time, could be just around the corner.

Goals are not achieved overnight. People talk about how much they appreciate the journey and all of the steps and stops along the way. It may not seem like an enjoyable experience when you are going through it but when you look back and focus on the good, you'll find that the journey just may be some of the best times in your life.

Unlimited; everything is.

-- D. Alexander Griffin

P = PHYSICAL

Physical (fiz/I kel) *(Merriam-Webster)*

1. of or pertaining to the body.

2. of or pertaining to that which is material: the physical universe.

3. noting or pertaining to the properties of matter and energy other than those peculiar to living matter.

4. carnal; sexual: physical attraction.

5. requiring characterized by, or liking rough physical contact or strenuous physical activity.

Physical relates to what will motivate your body. With positive *physical* motivation you can achieve things with your body you never thought possible. Our body is an extension of our minds and with that information we know we can ultimately control what our body does.

People talk about body language and how they can read a person's mood by looking at signs or signals that person's body is giving off. I remember an excerpt from the Peanuts™ cartoon where Charlie Brown was being his usual self and was feeling down about life but found that if he stood up straight and walked confidently it was impossible to feel down.

Although your mind controls your body, your body can be taught to remember certain commands and act almost instinctually. This is basically like a physical cruise control. Just like cardio or weight training, positive physical repetition is an extremely effective form of motivation and is a manifestation of you putting your goals into action.

My Pathway

The Plan

In high school I never thought there was an option for me not to go to college. I knew college was super expensive and I didn't want to put all of that burden on my parents. That meant I needed to get a scholarship. I was a decent student, but definitely not a lock for Harvard. The possibility for an academic scholarship was definitely a long shot for me.

I thought my best bet at that time was to try and get an athletic scholarship and so I threw myself into sports. In my mind, it was only a matter of time before I would be playing basketball in the NBA. I had it all planned out. I was going to lead my high school team to two state championships. Get a scholarship to either Georgetown to play for John Thompson, UNLV to play for Jerry Tarkanian, or North Carolina and play for Dean Smith. The problem was, I wasn't starting on the varsity team and was just a hair over 5'11 inches. I was quick and athletic but not very skilled. I couldn't really shoot the ball and my footwork was terrible. Needless to say, there wasn't any recruiters sending me letters or knocking on my door.

At the end of my sophomore year, I still had dreams of playing in the NBA, but I found something else that I thought just might give me a chance to get a scholarship.

The Solution

One day in the spring after school, some friends and I were hanging out as we watched our track team get ready for practice. One of my friends who wasn't shy about his abilities, started talking trash to the track guys and before we all knew it, we were lined up in the grass to race. Not sure how I got roped into it, but if my buddy was in it, I had to be in the mix. I remember my buddy was wearing khakis on and I was wearing jeans and penny loafers. We beat the track guys in there running shoes and shorts, by a significant margin. At that point, I knew I had a chance to be good at something. I decided to run track my junior year and our team won the State Championships and I had 3 gold medals in the relays. I was excited about what I could potentially do in my senior year.

The thought of getting a track scholarship was still a long shot. I would have to win some individual races and run some really fast times to get noticed. There were two big obstacles in my way. One was since the track season was in the spring, I would have to wait until the very end of my senior year to know if I had a chance to get a scholarship. And two, track scholarships were scarce because it's not a well-funded sport in college. And because of the number of athletes needed to make up a team, they had to split up the scholarships. Most team members are only awarded partial scholarships.

After telling to one of our assistant coaches, Mr. Richardson, about my dream and he gave me some advice that changed my life. He said, don't wait for colleges to notice you, reach out and write directly to track coaches. He said my letter should introduce myself and have my times and grades so when it was time to run track in my senior year, I could possibly be on their radar. Another good bit of advice he gave me was to "cast a wide net," meaning I should write to any and every college that I might want to go to.

The summer before my senior year of high school, I spent hours in the library looking up schools with academic programs I was interested in, good track programs and the track coaches contact information for the coaches. I sent out more than 100 letters hoping that at least would show an interest in me of I just need one coach to show interest.

The Realization

My senior year was fun in basketball. We had a great team that had the perfect amount of grit and finesse. Our practices were so ultra-competitive that when it came to the games, most other teams couldn't even come close to matching our intensity. That year we made it all the way to the state finals but came up short. I had come to the realization early in the season that I wasn't going to get a scholarship to play basketball so I played freely. I took chances, gambled on steals and did everything I could to help my teammates shine. All of the pressure I may have put on myself was lifted. I knew I was probably not going to get that scholarship to a division one college so if any of my friends could, I was going to do everything I could to encourage and help them.

Realistically, my dream to play college basketball were over. I was okay with that because I was excited about the track and field season and what opportunities it could bring. I've always heard that when one door shuts, look around because another one could be unlocked and ready to be opened.

At this time, I had started to get some letters back from the school and track coaches that I had written to in the past summer. This gave me one of the most important things in life, hope. I knew that if I had a great senior year of track, I had a chance to be a college athlete. My senior year of track started off with a bang. I won my first few races and was getting faster each race. Then came the moment that helped me realize my dream. We had a track meet at the local college track. All of the high schools in the state were going to be there and some high schools from out of state. It was my opportunity to show off all of the hard work I had put in leading up to that point.

The Race

Since I had won a few races locally I just knew that I would be in the fastest heat of the 100-meter dash. Then it happened, I looked for my name and what lane I would be in and didn't see it. My good friend, who I mentioned before was also fast was in the race, but I wasn't. That was the race that everyone was going to be watching and I wasn't going to be in it. I wasn't going to get my chance to race against the best in the area. I was initially bummed, but then I started to feel like I was being disrespected. How could they not put me in that race? Was it because my coaches didn't think I was good enough? Was it because my times were not worthy of being in a race against the best? My single goal was to get a scholarship in track and I needed races like these to prove myself. I was filled with emotions that started to feel overwhelming. Then it happened. I used those emotions, those feelings as motivation for my goals. I thought if I could just focus on my race and run a time, I thought I could run. It wouldn't matter which race I was in. I would be able to make a statement that would translate into something special. I could only control my performance and I felt like if I could dominate, it wouldn't matter what heat I was in, I would still be successful. I then focused on dominating the field of runners I was racing. It wasn't about winning the race; it was about crushing anyone that lined up against me. I wasn't just winning; I was winning by a huge margin of victory.

As I was getting ready to run and looked at the other runners, they had no idea of my intentions and how they fit into my new found motivation.

They didn't know that they were just in the way of what I wanted to ultimately achieve. I was using this new motivation as fuel to change my thoughts of being disrespected into something positive. I'm sure they probably were thinking similar thoughts but I had this motivation built up in me for so long, I wasn't going to be denied.

Since I started high school, I realized that I had to give everything I could possibly give to achieve my goals. I knew I had to take this positive mental attitude into every possible opportunity I had because you never know how many chances you will actually get.

I used to hear that if you should always shoot for the stars because even if you don't make it, you are still in the heavens.

When the gun went off, I shot out of the blocks like a cannon. Halfway through the race I was so far in the front I couldn't feel any racers around me. I thought it wasn't because I was running fast but because I wasn't in the fastest race. I started to imaging someone in front of me that was going after my dream and I was not going to let them beat me. I was running out in front by myself but in my mind, I was last and had to catch everyone. To this day I have carried that mentality in everything I do.

I won the race!

After I finished and gathered my clothes, I found a spot to rest and watch the race I thought I belonged in. My teammate won the race and I was happy for him. If I couldn't prove myself against those elite racers the next best thing was my friend would.

After the race, I was listening to the top eight times for the 100 meters. When they got to number five, I felt great because maybe I could still have one of the top times. Then they got to number three and I was starting to feel bad because I thought I didn't even run fast enough to be in the top eight runners.

Then it happened, they said I had won with the fastest time in the state. I was filled with joy and confirmation that I belonged.

What I remembered most from that day was not that I was disappointed that I wasn't in the fastest heat of the race but that won the race against the best competitors. I turned my disappointment into positive energy. I remember I won the ultimate race; the race against myself.

Physical Quotes

Your mind and body are one unit.

Greatness

To be a great champion you must believe you are the best. If you're not, pretend you are.

-- Muhammad Ali

I was told over and over again that I would never be successful, that I was not going to be competitive and the technique was simply not going to work. All I could do was shrug and say 'We'll just have to see'.

-- Dick Fosbury

You owe it to yourself to be the best you can possibly be - in baseball and in life.

-- Pete Rose

"Obstacles don't have to stop you. If you run into a wall, don't turn around and give up. Figure out how to climb it, go through it, or work around it."

-- Michael Jordan

It's lack of faith that makes people afraid of meeting challenges, and I believed in myself.

-- Muhammad Ali

Ask not what your teammates can do for you. Ask what you can do for your teammates.

-- Magic Johnson

You have to expect things of yourself before you can do them.

-- Michael Jordan

When you're playing for the national championship, it's not a matter of life or death. It's more important than that.

-- Duffy Daugherty

"What to do with a mistake: recognize it, admit it, learn from it, forget it."

-- Dean Smith

I learned that if you want to make it bad enough, no matter how bad it is, you can make it.

-- Gale Sayers

You've got to take the initiative and play your game. In a decisive set, confidence is the difference.

-- Chris Evert

"You must not only have competitiveness but ability, regardless of the circumstance you face, to never quit."

-- Abby Wambach

"I've missed more than 9,000 shots in my career. I've lost almost 300 games. Twenty-six times I've been trusted to take the game-winning shot and missed. I've failed over and over and over again in my life. And that is why I succeed."

-- Michael Jordan

"Just believe in yourself. Even if you don't pretend that you do and, at some point, you will."

-- Venus Williams

"If something stands between you and your success, move it. Never be denied."

-- Dwayne "The Rock" Johnson

My motto was always to keep swinging. Whether I was in a slump or feeling badly or having trouble off the field, the only thing to do was keep swinging.

-- Hank Aaron

"I hated every minute of training, but I said, 'Don't quit. Suffer now and live the rest of your life as a champion.'"

-- Muhammad Ali

You miss 100 percent of the shots you don't take.

-- Wayne Gretzky

"I always felt that my greatest asset was not my physical ability, it was my mental ability."

-- Bruce Jenner

One does not become great by claiming greatness.

-- African saying

The penalty of success is to be bored by the attentions of people who formerly snubbed you.

-- Mary Wilson Little

If you fall, fall on your back. If you can look up, you can get up.

-- Les Brown

Sports do not build character...they reveal it.

-- John Wooden

To succeed...You need to find something to hold on to, something to motivate you, something to inspire you.

-- Tony Dorsett

"Baseball is the only field of endeavor where a man can succeed three times out of ten and be considered a good performer."

-- Ted Williams

Ingenuity, plus courage, plus work, equals miracles.

-- Bob Richards

"Persistence can change failure into extraordinary achievement."

-- Marv Levy

"Champions keep playing until they get it right."

-- Billie Jean King

"You are never really playing an opponent. You are playing yourself, your own highest standards, and when you reach your limits, that is real joy."

-- Arthur Ashe

Adversity causes some men to break; others to break records.

-- William A. Ward

Other people may not have had high expectations for me... but I had high expectations for myself.

-- Shannon Miller

When someone tells me there is only one way to do things, it always lights a fire under my butt. My instant reaction is, I'm gonna prove you wrong.

-- Picabo Street

"Some people say I have attitude – maybe I do...but I think you have to. You have to believe in yourself when no one else does – that makes you a winner right there."

-- Venus Williams

The best and fastest way to learn a sport is to watch and imitate a champion.

-- Jean-Claude Killy

"I never left the field saying I could have done more to get ready and that gives me peace of mind."

-- Peyton Manning

I've always made a total effort, even when the odds seemed entirely against me. I never quit trying; I never felt that I didn't have a chance to win.

-- Arnold Palmer

I skate to where the puck is going to be, not where it has ben.

-- Wayne Gretzky

Sportsmanship

Either lead, follow, or get out of the way.

There's only one way to succeed in anything, and that is to give it everything. I do, and I demand that of my players.

-- Vince Lombardi

It's what you learn after you know it all that counts.

-- John Wooden

It is amazing what can be accomplished when nobody cares about who gets the credit.

-- Robert Yates

When you're playing against a stacked deck, compete even harder. Show the world how much you'll fight for the winner's circle. If you do, someday the cellophane will crackle off a fresh pack, one that belongs to you, and the cards will be stacked in your favor.

-- Pat Riley

The difference between a successful person and others is not a lack of strength, not a lack of knowledge, but rather a lack of will.

-- Vincent T. Lombardi

"Do you know what my favorite part of the game is? The opportunity to play."

-- Mike Singletary

There's no substitute for guts.

-- Paul Bear Bryant

The game of life is a lot like football. You have to tackle your problems, block your fears and score your points when you get the opportunity.

-- Lewis Grizzard

Most people give up just when they're about to achieve success. They quit on the one-yard line. They give up at the last minute of the game, one foot from a winning touchdown.

-- Ross Perot

"Leadership, like coaching, is fighting for the hearts and souls of men and getting them to believe in you."

-- Eddie Robinson

The way a team plays as a whole determines its success. You may have the greatest bunch of individual stars in the world, but if they don't play together, the club won't be worth a dime.

-- Babe Ruth

If you are not big enough to lose, you are not big enough to win.

-- Walter Reuther

If you don't have confidence, you'll always find a way not to win.

-- Carl Lewis

"If you have everything under control, you're not moving fast enough."

-- Mario Andretti

It's not the size of the dog in the fight, but the size of the fight in the dog.

-- Archie Griffen

"Never give up, never give in, and when the upper hand is ours, may we have the ability to handle the win with the dignity that we absorbed the loss."

-- Doug Williams

The minute you start talking about what you're going to do if you lose, you have lost.

-- George Schultz

Setting a goal is not the main thing. It is deciding how you will go about achieving it and staying with that plan.

-- Tom Landry

"What makes something special is not just what you have to gain, but what you feel there is to lose."

-- Andre Agassi

Each of us has a fire in our heart for something. It's our goal in life to find it and to keep it lit.

-- Mary Lou Retton

If you set a goal for yourself and are able to achieve it, you have won your race. Your goal can be to come in first, to improve your performance, or just finish the race it's up to you.

-- Dave Scott

Right or wrong, good or bad, you gotta love sports.

-- Anonymous

"Most talented players don't always succeed. Some don't even make the team. It's more what's inside."

-- Brett Favre

It's hard to beat a person who never gives up.

-- Babe Ruth

I'll always be Number 1 to myself.

-- Moses Malone

If a man can beat you, walk him.

-- Leroy "Satchel" Paige

Don't measure yourself by what you have accomplished, but by what you should have accomplished with your ability.

-- John Wooden

Be strong in body, clean in mind, lofty in ideals.

-- Dr. James Naismith

How you respond to the challenge in the second half will determine what you become after the game, whether you are a winner or a loser.

-- Lou Holtz

"Wisdom is always an overmatch for strength."

-- Phil Jackson

Perhaps the single most important element in mastering the techniques and tactics of racing is experience. But once you have the fundamentals, acquiring the experience is a matter of time.

-- Greg LeMond

Do not let what you cannot do interfere with what you can do.

-- John Wooden

One man can be a crucial ingredient on a team, but one man cannot make a team.

-- Kareem Abdul-Jabbar

"Never give up! Failure and rejection are only the first step to succeeding."

-- Jim Valvano

I know that I'm never as good or bad as any single performance. I've never believed my critics or my worshippers, and I've always been able to leave the game at the arena.

-- Charles Barkley

The game isn't over till it's over.

-- Yogi Berra

"Don't be afraid of failure. This is the way to succeed."

-- LeBron James

There are only two options regarding commitment. You're either IN or you're OUT. There's no such thing as life "in between."

-- Pat Riley

Willpower

There may be people that have more talent than you, but there's no excuse for anyone to work harder than you do.

-- Derek Jeter

The difference between the impossible and the possible lies in a person's determination.

-- Tommy Lasorda

You win some, you lose some, and some get rained out, but you gotta suit up for them all.

-- J. Askenberg

"Somewhere behind the athlete you've become and the hours of practice and the coaches who have pushed you is a little girl who fell in love with the game and never looked back... play for her."

-- Mia Hamm

If you train hard, you'll not only be hard, you'll be hard to beat.

-- Herschel Walker

Luck is what happens when preparation meets opportunity.

-- Seneca

"If you can't outplay them, outwork them."

-- Ben Hogan

You learn you can do your best even when it's hard, even when you're tired and maybe hurting a little bit. It feels good to show some courage.

-- Joe Namath

"The more difficult the victory, the greater the happiness in winning."

-- Pele

"Most people never run far enough on their first wind to find out they've got a second."

-- William James

The five S's of sports training are: stamina, speed, strength, skill, and spirit; but the greatest of these is spirit.

-- Ken Doherty

Nothing will work unless you do.

-- John Wooden

"Continuous effort — not strength or intelligence — is the key to unlocking our potential."

-- Liane Cardes

"Age is no barrier. It's a limitation you put on your mind."

-- Jackie Joyner-Kersee

Set you goals high, and don't stop til you get there.

-- Bo Jackson

Winning is a habit. Unfortunately, so is losing.

-- Vince Lombardi

Show me a guy who's afraid to look bad, and I'll show you a guy you can beat every time.

-- Lou Brock

It's not necessarily the amount of time you spend at practice that counts; it's what you put into the practice.

-- Eric Lindros

Even if at first you do succeed, you still have to work hard to stay there.

-- Richard C. Miller

Don't look back. Something might be gaining on you.

-- Leroy "Satchel" Paige

Winning isn't everything, wanting to is.

-- Vince Lombardi

The mind is the limit. As long as the mind can envision the fact that you can do something, you can do it as long as you really believe 100 percent.

-- Arnold Schwarzenegger

Potential means – you ain't doing nothing now.

-- Michelle Ventour

Physical Pounds:

1) What you eat in private you wear in public.

2) I will lose weight because I've finally figured out who I am...and I'm not fat.

3) I am going to do it. No doubt. No excuses.

4) Practice safe eating. Always use condiments.

5) Vegetables are your friends!

6) If your dog is overweight, you're not exercising enough.

7) Where the mind goes the rear end follows.

8) Learning to lose is like basic training, but maintaining the desired weight is the real battleground.

9) I love myself more than I love food.

10) Today is the fattest day of the rest of my life

11) It's hard to be fit as a fiddle when you are shaped like a cello.

12) If you value your hopes and dreams more than you value eating...YOU WILL MAKE IT.

13) Never eat more than you can lift.

14) Step away from that doughnut and no one gets hurt.

15) Weight Watchers is like the mob. You can never really leave because you'll always know too much.

16) A year from now you'll wish you had started today.

-- Unknown

Strength does not come from physical capacity. It comes from an indomitable will.

-- Mahatma Gandhi

The principle is competing against yourself. It's about self-improvement, about being better than you were the day before.

-- Steve Young

"It's going to be a journey. It's not a sprint to get in shape."

-- Kerri Walsh Jennings

"It is more difficult to stay on top than to get there."

-- Mia Hamm

"If you persevere long enough, if you do the right things long enough, the right things will happen."

-- Manon Rheaume

"It doesn't matter what you're trying to accomplish. It's all a matter of discipline."

-- Wilma Rudolph

"Gold medals aren't really made of gold. They're made of sweat, determination, and a hard-to-find alloy called guts."

-- Dan Gable

If you don't do what's best for your body, you're the one who comes up on the short end.

-- Julius Erving

A man too busy to take care of his health is like a mechanic too busy to take care of his tools.

-- Spanish proverb

Good friends are good for your health.

--Irwin Sarason

Laughter is the most healthful exertion.

-- Christoph Wilhelm Hufeland

You only have one life. What body do you want to live it in?

-- Anonymous

"The only person who can stop you from reaching your goals is you."

-- Jackie Joyner-Kersee

Visualize = Realize

I'm a visual person. One way I help myself set goals and stay focused is to set visual cues all around me. When I was running track in college, my coach introduced us to visualization. He would have us all lay down in a room and close our eyes and only focus on his voice. The process would start with him having us focus on a single part of our body and flex the muscles around it. We would start at our feet. We would flex the muscles around it; hold the muscles tight, then release all of the energy around it. We would then move up through our legs, flexing our calves, thighs and hamstrings. Then we would flex our midsection including our stomach muscles, chest and back. This exercise would continue through our arms, up to our neck and back down through all of our muscles, ending at our feet where we began.

By then our body was completely relaxed and we were ready for visualization. He would talk about the all of the aspects of our races from the start through the drive phase and how we would feel effortlessly running at our top speed down the track. We would not only visualize running the perfect race, but also the feeling we would have accomplishing our ultimate goal. Winning the race.

At first, I thought this was kind of silly. I let my mind wander to things that didn't have anything to do with racing. I would think about how hard school was, why my friends seemed to be having more fun at school than I was and what I was going to wear to the next party.

I wanted to be a better runner, but I didn't know how. I tried to workout harder, lift weight longer, but I wasn't achieving the goals or times I had hoped for. The things I was doing to get better were a step in the right direction, but just like any race, you still have to finish. I needed something that could help me get over the hump and finish the race as strong as I started it.

It took me many times going through this process to truly appreciate the power of visualization and how it could help me accomplish my goals. Once I committed to it, I was able to see what the next steps were to get me where I wanted to be. I wanted so badly to win races but there was something getting in my way. I had to see myself winning the races and believe I could, before I could actually do it.

Visualization was what helped me get to the realization I was seeking.

I started to use other methods of visualization to program my mindset. I made cardboard signs that I put around my apartment with the times I wanted to run. Everywhere I would look there was a reminder of what success for me would look like.

This was subliminally programing my goals in my mind. After a while I didn't even see the posters, but I knew they were there and my mind was taking account.

I started watching big races with runners who looked like me winning races. I would pause the races to study everything from body positions to number of steps to each key phase of the race to proximity of the other racers. In my mind I knew what I should be doing at every point of the race. I watch the same races over and over to a point that when I was going through my visualization sessions, I had a clear picture in my mind of what success looked like. This helped me in my real races to the point of every moment in the race, seemed familiar. I felt like I had been there before and was confident of what was going to happen next.

Another part of visualization is how the spoken word ties into your mental thoughts. I would talk to myself and say out loud cues that would ingrain in my mind the things I needed for success. I would say, "drive, drive, drive." Or "lift your knees and stand up and float to the finish." I would incorporate this all throughout my day; sometimes saying "knees, knees" as I was walking to class. I'm sure other students probably were looking at me crazy but I didn't care. If I wanted to be successful, I had to fully commit. This not only reinforced what steps I needed to take to achieve my goals, but also helped me build up the anticipation of what I was going to do when I had the chance.

To go along with the idea of how the spoken word helps with my motivation was what I call putting your goals into the universe. You can't just keep them to yourself. I believe that if you want to achieve you goals you have to create accountability. One way to do that is to tell people what your goals are. You should communicate your goals to friends, family or anyone who will listen. This gives you an added motivation because now you have communicated what you plan to do and you definitely don't want to let anyone else down. Some think of it as added pressure but I think it's an essential part of fully committing to your goals. When other people know your goals are, once you realize them, it becomes even more satisfying.

Learn when it's time to focus and when you can let your mind go; you will accomplish tasks more quickly and feel more rested in between.

-- D. Alexander Griffin

S = SPIRITUAL

Spiritual (spir/I choo el) *(Merriam-Webster)*

1. pertaining to the spirit or soul, as distinguished from the physical nature.
2. of or pertaining to the spirit as the seat of the moral or religious nature.
3. of or pertaining to sacred things or matters; religious.
4. pertaining to or consisting of spirit; incorporeal.
5. closely akin in interests, outlook feeling, etc.: the composer's spiritual heir.
6. pertaining to spirits or to spiritualists; supernatural or spiritualistic.

Your spiritual health is the base of all motivation.

Your spiritual health is the most powerful motivation because it stems from what you believe in. With a strong belief you can basically do anything you could ever dream up. Throughout history there is talk of pioneers who were fearless, innovative, or brilliant. The one thing all of these people have in common is their belief system (spirit). Your belief system could stem from a religious base, your personal thoughts on what is right or wrong, your own inner spirituality or any combination of the above.

Your spirit is your life force and it can be on a good path or a bad path. In many cases your spirit is not on a path at all and that's when you fall into a place some people refer to as limbo. Some people spend their whole life in limbo and they are fine with that. These people don't care about making a difference or changing the world, just what's going on in their personal world. Your spirit dictates the presence of your mind and body and how it affects everything around you.

Take time to feed your spiritual health. Use meditation to think of your goals and identify the thing you believe in. The things you feel strongly about. These things build up your belief system around what you can accomplish in life. You only have to believe it, to achieve it.

Spirituality

Spirituality is something that has many different meanings to many different people. Spirituality could be a feeling, a practice or a state of mind, just to name a few. With that said, everyone had their own personal feeling that goes with the word spiritual. I think everyone's own view of spirituality is perfect for them.

Some people say religion is their gateway to spirituality. They use religion and spirituality synonymously. One of the things our country was built on was freedom of religion. And believe me, I know about religion.

I grew up in a bi-religious house hold; half Lutheran and half Baptize. So of course, most Sundays I was in church. The basic principles of the two religions were similar, but how they were practiced were slightly different. I enjoyed both and learned to embrace the differences. They both motivated me spiritually in different ways.

One of the religions used structure and repetition that created a familiarity that I found comfort in. I knew what was going to happen and be talked about throughout the year on a seasonal basis. My Lutheran experience is filled with hymns and sayings that I memorized over the course of my life that I when I think about and recite it is like a meditation. The repetition and rhythmic cadence take me to a place where I am comfortable and feel safe. And just like with any repetition, it's a form of practice and we all know practice makes perfect.

The other religion spoke to my spirituality on more of an emotional basis. The structure was built on what would move the congregation into participation. There was a focus on life experiences that people could relate to. Whether it was current events or situations, it was something that everyone could easily relate to and triggered a deep feeling. I knew that when I was engaging, my emotions would be triggered whether happy or sad but ultimately there was always a crescendo and I would leave with a feeling of hope.

I definitely cherished both experiences and keep them close to me so when needed, I can call upon them to get me through tough times.

Freedom of spirituality, no matter what you believe in or not believe in, is essential in your journey towards your goals. It's the ultimate motivation. When you think of that little voice in your head that drives you get up or keep going. You can find comfort in that voice as your spirit having an intimate, personal conversation with you. Feeling like you have freedom of spirituality is the purest form of inner peace and motivation.

Spiritual Quotes

Spirit is a fancy name for your "sole." It's only...and all of you.

Lessons

What you do not want others to do to you, do not do to others.

-- Confucius (circa 500 B.C.)

When you are kind to someone in trouble, you hope they'll remember and be kind to someone else. And it'll become like a wildfire.

-- Whoopi Goldberg

When you strengthen your self-esteem, there is no room for jealousy.

-- Dr. Harold Bloomfield

A disciple having asked for a definition of charity, the Master said LOVE ONE ANOTHER.

-- Confucius

Everything that is done in the world is done by hope.

-- Dr. Martin Luther King, Jr.

Do for others just what you want them to do for you.

-- The Good News Bible, Luke 6:31

Do all the good you can By all the means you can In all the ways you can In all the places you can At all times you can To all the people you can As long as you can.

-- Bernard Meltzer

It's ironic, but until you can free those final monsters within the jungle of yourself, your life, your soul is up for grabs.

-- Rona Barrett

Let us be of good cheer, remembering that the misfortunes hardest to bear are those that will never happen.

--James Russell Lowell

In a moment of decision, the best thing you can do is the right thing to do. The worst thing you can do is nothing.

-- Theodore Roosevelt

Never talk defeat. Use words like hope, belief, faith, victory.

-- Norman Vincent Peale

People will forget what you said. People will forget what you did...but people will never forget how you made them feel.

-- Maya Angelou

When you forgive, you in no way change the past but you sure do change the future.

-- Bernard Meltzer

The good you do today may be quickly forgotten, but the impact of what you do will never disappear.

-- Anonymous

True friendship is like sound health; the value of it is seldom known until it is lost.

-- Charles Caleb Colton

The person who seeks to change another person in a relationship basically sets the stage for a great deal of conflict

-- Wesley Snipes

To have a good life, it is not enough to remove what is wrong with it. We also need a positive goal, otherwise, why keep going?

-- Mihaly Csikszentmihalyi

A careless word may kindle strife; a cruel word may wreck a life; a timely word may level stress; a loving word may heal and bless.

-- Anonymous

Shall we make a new rule of life from tonight: always try to be a little kinder than is necessary.

-- Sir James M. Barrie

Thoughts from the Dalai Llama

1) Take into account that great love and great achievements involve great risk.

2) When you lose, don't lose the lesson.

3) Follow the 3 Rs: Respect for self, Respect for others and Responsibility for all your actions.

4) Remember that not getting what you want is sometimes a wonderful stroke of luck.

5) Learn the rules so you know how to break them properly.

6) Don't let a little dispute injure a great friendship.

7) When you realize you've made a mistake, take immediate steps to correct it.

8) Spend some time alone every day.

9) Open your arms to change, but don't let it change your values.

10) Remember that silence is sometimes the best answer.

11) Live a good, honorable life. Then when you get older and think back, you'll be able to enjoy it a second time.

12) A loving atmosphere in your home is the foundation for your life.

13) In disagreements with loved ones, deal only with the current situation. Don't bring up the past.

14) Share your knowledge. It's a way to achieve immortality.

15) Be gentle with the earth.

16) Once a year, go someplace you've never been before.

17) Remember that the best relationship is one in which your love for each other exceeds your need for each other.

18) Judge your success by what you had to give up in order to get it.

19) Approach love and cooking with reckless abandon.

Life's most persistent and urgent question is, what are you doing for others?

-- Martin Luther King, Jr.

Your talent is God's gift to you. What you do with it is your gift back to God.

-- Leo Buscaglia

Take a day to heal from the lies you've told yourself and the ones that have been told to you.

-- Maya Angelou

And as we let our own light shine, we unconsciously give other people permission to do the same. As we are liberated from our own fear, our presence automatically liberates others.

-- Nelson Mandela

Enlightenment

Today is called the "present" because it is a gift from God.

-- Sri as Ravi Shankar

Blessed are those who give without remembering. And blessed are those who take without forgetting.

-- Bernard Meltzer

You are a child of God. You playing small does not serve the world. There is nothing enlightened about shrinking so that other people won't feel in- secure about you. We were born to manifest the glory of God that is within us.

-- Nelson Mandela

Ask, and it shall be given you...

-- The Holy Bible, Matthew 7:7

Fear less, hope more; eat less, chew more; whine less, breathe more; talk less, say more; hate less, love more and all good things are yours.

-- Swedish Proverb

For unto whomsoever much is given, of him shall much be required...

-- The Holy Bible, Luke 12:48

The moment you move out of the way, you make room for a miracle to take place.

-- Dr. Barbara King

The most sacred place isn't the church, the mosque, or the temple, it's the temple of the body. That's where spirit lives.

-- Susan Taylor

If we stand tall it is because we stand on the backs of those who came before us.

-- Yoruba proverb

Don't let anyone steal your spirit.

-- Sinbad

God is always capable of making something out of nothing.

-- The Honorable Minister Louis Farrakhan

Look not back in anger, nor forward in fear but around you in awareness.

-- Ross Hersey

Nothing can dim the light which shines from within.

-- Maya Angelou

If you want to lift yourself up, lift up someone else.

-- Booker T. Washington

When you are not happy with yourself, you cannot be happy with others.

-- Daryl Mitchell

Talent is God given. Be humble. Fame is man-given. Be grateful. Conceit is self-given. Be

careful.

-- John Wooden

The happiest of people don't necessarily have the best of everything; they just make the most of everything that comes their way.

-- Unknown

He who wishes to secure the good of others has already secured his own.

-- Confucius.

Our greatest problems in life come not so much from the situations we confront as from our doubts about our ability to handle them.

-- Susan Taylor

There are only two ways to live your life. One is as though nothing is a miracle. The other is as though everything is a miracle.

-- Albert Einstein

The nonviolent approach does not immediately change the heart of the oppressor. It first does something to the hearts and souls of those committed to it. It gives them new self-respect; it calls up resources of strength and courage that they did not know they had. Finally, it reaches the opponent and so stirs his conscience that reconciliation becomes a reality.

-- Martin Luther King, Jr.

If you would lift me up you must be on higher ground.

-- Ralph Waldo Emerson

Use the talents you possess: for the woods would be very silent if no birds sang except the best.

-- Henry van Dyke

When women have a voice in national and international affairs, wars will cease forever.

-- Augusta Stowe-Gullen

Only a life lived for others is worth living.

-- Albert Einstein

Tenderness and kindness are not signs of weakness and despair but manifestations of strength and resolution.

-- Kahil Gibran

Goodness is the only investment that never fails.

-- Henry David Thoreau

Where there is love there is life.

-- Mahatma Gandhi

Knowing others is wisdom. Knowing the self is enlightenment.

-- Lao-tzu

In the solitude of your mind are the answers to all your questions about life. You must take the time to ask and listen.

-- Bawa Mahaiyaddeen

Peace

Possession of material riches without inner peace is like dying of thirst while bathing in a river.

-- Parahansa Yogananda

Peace be with you.

-- The Holy Bible, Genesis 43:23

Peace starts with a smile.

-- Mother Teresa

Nothing can bring you peace but yourself.

-- Ralph Waldo Emerson

Until you make peace with who you are, you'll never be content with what you have.

-- Doris Mortman

If you cannot find peace within yourself, you will never find it anywhere else.

-- Marvin Gaye

If your spiritual philosophy is not moving you to the state of peace, health, wealth and love your spirit desires...you need a new spiritual philosophy.

-- Sun Bear

Happiness consists not of having much, but in being content with little.

--Marguerite, Countess of Blessington

Love is the only force capable of turning an enemy into a friend.

-- Martin Luther King, Jr.

A warm smile is the universal language of kindness.

-- William Arthur Ward

If my heart can become pure and simple, like that of a child, I think there probably can be no greater happiness than this.

-- Kitaro Nishida

Before you speak ask yourself if what you are going to say is true, is kind, is necessary, is helpful. If the answer is no, maybe what you are about to say should be left unsaid.

-- Bernard Meltzer

Porque el miedo, sin ser Dios, suele hacer algo de nada. (Fear can, though it is not God, create something from nothing.)

-- Caspar de Aguilar

If you plant turnips, you will not harvest grapes.

-- Akan proverb

Dreams

Each day brings you one step closer to your dreams coming true.

-- Anonymous

It is good to dream, but it is better to dream and work. Faith is mighty, but action with faith is mightier. Desiring is helpful, but work and desire are invincible.

-- Thomas Robert Gaines

Dreams come true; without that possibility, nature would not incite us to have them.

-- John Updike

"You dream. You plan. You reach. There will be obstacles. There will be doubters. There will be mistakes. But with hard work, with belief, with confidence and trust in yourself and those around you, there are no limits."

-- Michael Phelps

Consult not your fears but your hopes and your dreams. Think not about your frustrations, but about your unfulfilled potential. Concern yourself not with what you tried and failed in, but with what it is still possible for you to do.

-- Pope John XXIII

No amount of security is worth the suffering of a life lived chained to a routine that has killed your dreams.

-- Kent Nerburn

Nothing is as real as a dream. The world can change around you, but your dream will not. Responsibilities need not erase it. Duties need not obscure it. Because the dream is within you, no one can take it away.

-- Unknown

When you are inspired by some great purpose, some extraordinary project, all your thoughts break their bounds: your mind transcends limitations, your consciousness expands in every direction and you find yourself in a new, great and wonderful world....and you discover yourself to be a greater person by far than you ever dreamed yourself to be...

-- Patanjali

Life follows dreams. By giving up on your dreams you are giving up on life itself.

-- D. Alexander Griffin

Believe

Your belief determines your action and your action determines your results, but first you have to believe.

-- Mark Victor Hansen

It is this belief in a power larger than myself and other than myself which allows me to venture into the unknown and even the unknowable.

-- Maya Angelou

Our hearts are the wrapping which preserve God's word, we need no more.

-- The Koran, Sura 4:155

It is our own mental attitude which makes the world what it is for us. Our thoughts make things beautiful; our thoughts make things ugly. The whole world is in our own minds. Learn to see things in the proper light. First, believe in this world – that there is meaning behind everything. Everything in the world is good, is holy and beautiful. If you see something evil, think that you are not understanding it in the right light. Throw the burden on yourselves!

-- Swami Vivekananda

If you give 100%, God will make up the difference!

-- Anonymous

Heaven is where you'll be when you are okay right where you are.

-- Sun Ra

My religion is very simple. My religion is kindness.

-- The Dalai Lama

LENT = Let's Eliminate Negative Thinking.

-- Earl Nightingale

God made three requests for his children: do the best you can, where you are, with what you have, now.

-- African-American folklore

If God be for us, who can be against us?

-- Romans 8:31

Gray skies are just clouds passing over.

-- Duke Ellington

I will fear no evil: for thou art with me...

-- The Holy Bible, Psalm 23:4

Be careful what you hope for, you just might get it.

The remarkable thing about fearing God is that when you fear God you fear nothing else, whereas if you do not fear God you fear everything else.

-- Oswald Chambers

Everything that has to happen had to happen. Everything that must happen cannot be stopped.

-- Dwayne Dyer

God would not give us the ability and opportunity to be successful and then condemn us to mediocrity.

-- Debra Anderson

There is a soul force in the universe, which, if we permit it, will flow through us and produce miraculous results.

-- Mahatma Gandhi

When one door closes, another one opens.

-- African American folklore

The quality, not the longevity, of one's life is what is important.

-- Dr. Martin Luther King, Jr.

Spiritual growth results from absorbing and digesting truth and putting it into practice in daily life.

-- White Eagle

What God Will And Won't Ask

1)   God won't ask what kind of car you drove, but will ask how many people you drove who didn't have transportation.

2)   God won't ask the square footage of your house, but will ask how many people you welcomed into your home.

3)   God won't ask about the fancy clothes you had in your closet, but will ask how many of those clothes helped the needy.

4)   God won't ask about your social status, but will ask what kind of class you displayed.

5)   God won't ask how many material possessions you had, but will ask if they dictated your life.

6)   God won't ask what your highest salary was, but will ask if you compromised your character to obtain that salary.

7)   God won't ask how much overtime you worked, but will ask if you worked overtime for your family and loved ones.

8)   God won't ask how many promotions you received, but will ask how you promoted others.

9)   God won't ask what your job title was, but will ask if you performed your job to the best of your ability.

10)   God won't ask what you did to help yourself, but will ask what you did to help others.

11)   God won't ask how many friends you had, but will ask how many people to whom you were a true friend.

12)   God won't ask what you did to protect your rights, but will ask what you did to protect the rights of others.

13)   God won't ask in what neighborhood you lived, but will ask how you treated your neighbors.

14)   God won't ask about the color of your skin, but will ask about the content of your character.

15)   God won't ask how many times your deeds matched your words but will ask how many times they didn't.

-- Unknown

Faith is not belief without proof, but trust without reservation.

-- Elton Trueblood

Faith is not something to grasp, it is a state to grow into.

-- Mahatma Gandhi

Take the first step in faith. You don't have to see the whole staircase, just take the first step.

-- Dr. Martin Luther King, Jr.

All I have seen teaches me to trust the creator for all that I have not seen.

-- Ralph Waldo Emerson

I believe that unarmed truth and unconditional love will have the final word in reality. This is why right, temporarily defeated, is stronger that evil triumphant.

-- Martin Luther King Jr.

For with God nothing shall be impossible.

-- Luke 1:37

Enthusiasm is nothing more or less than faith in action.

-- Henry Chester

To sleep is an act of faith.

-- Barbara G. Harrison

Optimism is the faith that leads to achievement. Nothing can be done without hope or confidence.

-- Helen Keller

He who loses money, loses much; He who loses a friend, loses much more, He who loses faith, loses all.

-- Eleanor Roosevelt

That's the thing about faith. If you don't have it you can't understand it. And if you do, no explanation is necessary.

-- Major Kira Nerys

Faith is to believe what you do not see; the reward of this faith is to see what you believe.

-- St. Augustine

Faith can move mountains; doubt can create them.

-- Anonymous

Fear imprisons, faith liberates; fear paralyzes, faith empowers; fear disheartens, faith encourages; fear sickens, faith heals; fear makes useless, faith makes serviceable.

-- Harry Emerson Fosdick

Faith

"I don't necessarily have to see it to believe it but sometimes seeing it helps me get there faster."

This is a reality of life. Faith is knowing something or believing in something that you may not be able to see. Hence the saying "faith is blind." Blind faith is an engrained in our lives in many ways. It is a major staple in religion. Blind faith gives you hope and a purpose bigger than life itself. It helps you stay motivated without a physical object or thing to cling to. You can accomplish almost anything with faith. When trying to go where no one had gone before, you need to use faith as your main motivator.

But faith doesn't always have to be blind. You still have to keep your eyes and senses open in your journey to your goals or motivation You can seek out key markers that reenforce your faith. If someone else has done what you are trying to do or even came close to doing it. Your faith can get you over the edge. Sometimes there are signs or clues you can research that point you in the right direction. Kind of like a treasure map.

Treasure maps are hard to read and many times coded in a way you are not use to understanding. But once you crack your code, the path to the treasure is clear. This is something that may come quickly or take years to figure out.

Faith takes you on a journey to an unknown entity. You may not even know what that entity is but it's usually the reward you've been looking for.

"Have faith, young Skywalker."

-- Obi-Wan Kenobi

My Motivation...

I wrote this book as a way to come to terms with my demons of the past. Through the introspection I have conquered my fears, my negative thoughts. I have looked at my inner self and figured out what makes me tic. I have not only identified what motivates me for today but also what will motivate me in the future. I said in the beginning of my book that this started as a collection of motivational quotes that I would look at from time to time to help me keep my head up in tough situations. What I found was what gets me through life.

Everyone has special experiences in life that make them proud, that inspire and motivate them. These things ultimately contribute to their overall happiness. If life is about searching for those experiences, then life will continually be meaningful and worth every minute.

When people say; it's the little things that make them happy or that motivate them, I used to think "how cliché." But as I look around my world and I see a beautiful sunset, a breathtaking mountain silhouette, kids playing outside without a care in the world, or an older couple walking in the park holding hands. I take a deep breath, thank God and think, "isn't life awesome."

This is my motivation and I hope through this journey, it's your motivation too.

Peace!

Love, Grifman

Acknowledgments

First and foremost, I would like to thank God for empowering me to achieve all of my dreams.

I would like to thank my wife for always believing in me.

I would like to thank my mom for helping me become the person I am today.

I would like to thank my father for demonstrating to me what it takes to develop a strong work ethic.

I would like to thank my sister for being my inspiration along with being my advisor, legal counsel, manager, agent, my editor, etc...

I would also like to thank these important people who have influenced my life experiences: Roderick Bradley, Kevin Carroll, Patrick Collins, Shelly Davis, Kyla Egan, Darian Eliassen, Eric Love, Carlene Faessler, Wayne Fisher, Andrea Gaston, Gary Gates, Kathy Goods, Burdett Griffin, Gregory Griffin, Kendall Griffin, John Hess, Bernadette Hislop, Phillip Hubbard III, Brian Jansen, Neerig Mani, Yves McDavid, Dave Nielson, Mike O'dea, Sha Rhonda Ramos, Hezekiah Reed, Margaret Reed, Mr. Richardson, Charles Slater, Keith Turner, Lester Turner, and last but not least The Mighty Mighty Phi Beta Sigma.

About the author

Born Daniel Alexander Griffin Jr, in Chicago Illinois.

My first inspirational moment that I remember was when my family (father, mother, sister and I) sang a song entitled "Can you feel a brand-new day" by Luther Vandross, in Church. My entire family is musically gifted and I thought I was also.

Then there was that fatal piano recital bomb (my most embarrassing moment) in front of thousands of people, (okay hundreds) okay; maybe about 50 people, but it felt like thousands. The good thing that came out of that horrible experience is that I embraced my love and skill in athletics.

At age 13, my mother and I moved from Chicago to Las Vegas where I started to excel in sports. Although my mom and I didn't see eye to eye on many things, we made it through my rebellious teenage years. My mom was always giving me direction and I thought I knew it all. I received a track scholarship and attended Idaho State University where I received an undergraduate and graduate degree. While working on my master's degree full time, I was also an Athletic Advisor, an Assistant Track Coach and worked in the school's ticket booth. Throughout this time my only motivation was to have my family and friends be proud of me.

Then finally came the ultimate realization. My family and friends were already proud of me, and all that advice my mom gave me that I chose not to listen to, was actually right. Go figure!